# IN THESE MOUNTAINS

# IN THESE

COLLIER BOOKS/Macmillan Publishing Company    New York

# MOUNTAINS

## Peter Sacks

COLLIER MACMILLAN PUBLISHERS      London

Macmillan Publishing Company
866 Third Avenue, New York, N.Y. 10022
Collier Macmillan Canada, Inc.

Library of Congress Cataloging-in-Publication Data
Sacks, Peter M.
In these mountains.
I. Title.
PS3569.A235I5    1986      811'.54        85-29898
ISBN 0-02-070600-6

10 9 8 7 6 5 4 3 2 1

Designed by Jack Meserole

Printed in the United States of America

*In These Mountains* is also published in a hardcover edition
by Macmillan Publishing Company.

# CONTENTS

## ACKNOWLEDGMENTS

*Antioch Review*  FOR RICHARD TURNER
*Crazy Horse*  MACHADODORP; VALERIE
*Georgia Review*  CHANGE OF ADDRESS
*The Nation*  GIRAFFE
*The New Republic*  A VISIT TO THE HILLSTEAD MUSEUM; ARLES: THE BULLS
*The New Yorker*  KIRKPATRICK PLAYING BACH
*Partisan Review*  TRANSVAAL: UNDER FROST
*Seneca Review*  IN TIME; IN THESE MOUNTAINS


My special thanks to Kenneth Brecher, Douglas Livingstone, Frank and Dale Loy, David St. John, the Yaddo Corporation; and to Barbara Kassel, to whom this book is dedicated.

# IN THESE MOUNTAINS

## FRAGMENT—TO BARBARA

The sea, the wind, these quiet remains of Rome,
a quarry in the coastal rock, a hillside of carved stone;
names and dates I've not the means to recognize.

This afternoon, climbing above the sea,
I found a marble fragment scarcely buried in the dirt,
a small piece, say three fingers wide,

sharp ridges gathered toward a vanished knot—
a piece of pleated cloth torn from the intimate
close-fitting section of a woman's robe

emerging softly from the chisel. It seemed that I
were writing from the Spanish provinces to you in Rome,
the same sea washing bare the coastline,

washing at the netting of imperial intrigue—
an older, tidal sway. And then I saw that what I held
was not of marble, but a broken scallop shell,

its curve worn flat, the ridges drawing close
to what had been the cusp. Cast to this height,
a grey deposit grown stone-hard against one side,

it shows me, under the accumulated grit,
these ridges, like a lesson in perspective
almost meeting at the vanishing point—
the hard, straight, constant lines of love.

# PART I

# In Time

## ABOVE MASER

Above Maser, we climbed a private road
between low, fruitless olive trees, some
near-strangled by wild ivy, dark green
smothering the light. Behind them, vineyards
slanted upslope, swathes of new-cut grass
between each row—birdsong, insects drifting,
voices of the scythers somewhere to the side
as we slipped by unseeing and unseen.
The rise, a view of distant trees condensing
to a plush of greens while on the path ahead
a striped, red-crested woodpecker kept
shifting ground, a flash of plumage as
it flew a little further off each time.

Coming back, you walked ahead, stepping
carefully on the loose white pebbles,
your dress the slow green of the apple trees,
a warm breeze filling it out, filling
out the valley. Further down, the scythers
worked a furrow closer to the road, one
sharpening his blade, the whetstone holster open
at his belt. And you walked on into such
stillness I could barely follow more
than the soft larch leaves followed where
they hung in silence twisting in the light;
or than I follow now, passing where we stood
together for a moment in the unmown grass.

# A VISIT TO THE HILLSTEAD MUSEUM

Seventy years ago James queried where
in this bland New England purity
the people hid their passion.
Where beneath white steeples
in this unconfessing winter light
was what he called the "sensual margin,
overflow and by-play?"
Until he came upon this house,
discovering here a sudden blaze of art.

We, too, coming from the snow,
abruptly saw the Haystack paintings
burning on the wall—
the miraculous green shadow at the base of one,
another with that unexpected
stroke of mauve among the gold.

Looking then at Degas' pastel
of a woman bending in an iron tub,
whole landscapes of desire and distance
moulded in the contours of her back,
we saw the tints of light-
reflecting water at her feet
so that she seemed like Aphrodite
on a shallow sea at sunrise.

All this gathered.
Afterwards, we two were quiet,
turning less toward each other
than to future work.
But as we drove back
watching light fade from the whitest fields,
did you know how readily I would,
just that night, have left all work for pleasure,
and have carried the beauty of that day to you,
and to the body's first and ignorant embrace?

# IN TIME

Through six or seven dead elms
already labelled for removal,
we've watched the day slow-march
over the hills of Maryland
to a wind-ensemble of bird
calls dwindling in the breeze.

Now, in this darkened sun-porch,
awkward, empty-handed, you
and I turn east in talk
of other places, other times—
to Italy, the day we tramped through
vineyards of Brunello grapes
near Montalcino, and later,
toward nightfall, drank the long-
lived wine beside a church
laid out by Charlemagne
eleven centuries ago.

Inside the church, an old guide shone
his flashlight through an alabaster
column: "Now all translucent, see?
Once marble, then with age . . ."
a seam of luminosity
to hold against this night,
in which I wonder if the marble grew
transparent the way fruit
ripens, from the outside in,
and if the disappearing day,
even the passing bloom of light
behind the elms, caught up
and held in the right way,
in time, will see us through.

# ROME: FIRST NOTES

A city addicted to its own foundations,
walls becoming other walls
in an intricate labor of negotiations.

Column, cornice, tiled roof locking into
roof in a field of subdivided light,
each plane snagging the eye; an impromptu

earthenware conspiracy even the Italian
sun can't pacify. Before sunset
the clouds take on their Roman

colors—orange, Mars red, ochre—
travelling straight as though following the roads.
Below them, fork-tailed swifts scissor

the air or spin impatient for the seven hills,
for time as the herdsmen knew it—yellow straw,
a river, dust. An empire of details

in erosion, like the pale travertines
this city's built on, sedimentary as
each century's stain—each afternoon's.

# LINES FOR LAURENCE HOLLAND

*to Faith Holland*

It is an old custom, the griever calling
for another voice, antiphonal,
in which she may lay by her own lament
and yield to unaccustomed peace,
a borrowed calm that may become her own,
like evening in another land,
a far-off land, in which a softer light
falls on the traveller.

He moves among his own affections there,
at ease in a familiar region
fully found, a proven landscape as
of August fields, of wheat and wild-
flowers ripening.

And there, caught in that light
beyond bewilderment, he turns only
to accents calm enough to share his quietness,
the accents of a calmer grief,
a calm farewell, in which we find ourselves
almost beneath those skies
with him, as we will be—as we are now,
in the most quiet reaches of our lives.

# HENRY JAMES AND THE SEAL

Filling the air with pointless speculation,
we'd often thrown our hands up
during even the most perfect afternoons,
with the sea advancing coldly on the rocky mole,
or standing off completely at low tide. Until

one day, coming around the point,
we saw a seal, upright, less than twenty
yards offshore, the blunt head smooth
as any stone, whiskers spryly
fiddling the air, the grey slab
of his body vanishing into a wide
uncertainty of nonetheless clear water,
as though his very shape became
no more than waves of light
under the surface of the sea.

How suddenly we felt aroused
yet run aground there on the beach,
with the taste of exhaled air around us
and the flies buzzing about the seaweed
in the afternoon! And while
the seal basked and wavered in his element,
was it the sheer imbalance of our
certitudes against his play of ease
that laid us out so, without hope?

Whatever the truth, I tried
my hand at capturing the seal in some
indefinite world in which bright chances
offer themselves time and again;
but the wind blew on, the tide
erased the beach,
and the season overtook me.

So that recalling this would seem to be
a matter merely of renewing that surprise,
and that defeat, with less hold on the memory
than on the barest outline of a seal-like creature
somewhere in the loosened ebb and flow,
a compound now of what he was and of our
hesitating over him that day,
creating in our own delay
almost another coast he could inhabit,
drifting here and there
continually at bay.

# KIRKPATRICK PLAYING BACH

A white thread led him to the harpsichord,
and when he played we, too, were blind,
following nothing but the fugues
into a dazing of the ear,
where figures of a grand configuration rang
uncoiling through the all but deafened mind.

Coming out into the night, we listened
for an after-sound, as though the sky itself
might be a whispering bell.
The music had already folded
silently upon itself,
the player traced his way into the dark,
and we, like Echo in the quiet air, were left
to turn and return, fading until noiseless
as a coin sinking softly in a well.

# CHANGE OF ADDRESS

The cups already take
their rehooked angle,
hanging reflections
of the kitchen lights,
while the teapot's in dry dock
once more steaming pinkly nowhere
on its wooden shelf.
Even the casual fern is still
within its scribble.

How easily they cut us loose,
the cat already settling,
after his perfunctory exploration,
to an ever deeper mockery
of meditation:
"The *subject* of my reverie
may be death,
its *aim* is surely
sleep and a forgetting."

No use positioning, say,
a picture or a vase
as though to end all
motion in the momentary
stillness of a gaze.
Unsettled, half-unpacked,
you and I set off before dark
following a road at random
through the tall wet grass,
the fireflies seen
only as they glow
in tenses of their own,
a kind of future present now.

# ITS WAY HOME

A winter storm. Our Air New England
nineteen-seater rocking on the runway
like a dragonfly. The captain's voice,
"Our flying time to Waterville . . ."

As a child I took the wind
to be the motion of the earth,
but never could explain the windless days,
except to think we'd floated into calm at last,
the still water of time;
until the wind returned,
the earth took up its spin
with the child half-certain still
that in some weatherless sky
we might have moved with a forgotten ease.

Yet now, years later, buckled into flight
against the wind, are we approaching
some unforeseen exit in the air,
watching whatever recollections
might have bound us to return
fall with the falling earth?

Say Greece that noon on the far side of Spetsai,
following a track into the light,
into a bowl of green and gold,
the noise of light, as though I'd stumbled
on a concourse of forgotten voices
humming in the olives and the pines.
Or swimming off Cape Sounion
past the furthest rocks to look
back at Poseidon's temple black
against the sun.

The island drifts, the temple disappears,
the plane tilts in a rolling sky.
I set the nozzle of fresh air
against my face, its stream
dispersing through the mind
like shattered lights,
one last disintegration rising,
just as from a wreck
the trapped air, green and silver,
forces its way home.

# PART II

# News from Home

# BAMBOO

*When the emotions are strong and one*
*feels pent up, one should paint bamboo.*
—Chueh Yin

But what if one can neither paint nor draw,
and would arrive more at a blotting out
than at a graceful sweep of branch and leaf
against a paper sky?

Chueh Yin, is it enough to think of bamboo,
recollecting those of childhood
leaning there beyond the house
in another country?

To hear them creaking
thirty feet above the mound,
and to remember wedging up
between the tapering shafts
until they'd bend too far apart?

For hours I could sway up there
with the long thin streaming leaves,
gripping the yellow shine with either arm
to sail eastward in the offshore wind,
departing then—as now against a paper sky.

# FOR RICHARD TURNER

*Assassinated in Durban, South Africa, January 8, 1978*

You wrote on the pack page
of my last essay ("Political
Education in *The Republic*")
"Good ideas, but style
too literary. Use of images
evades the final point."

When I left,
you thought me still evasive,
trying to pass off
my own fear of suffering
as a form of wisdom.
I'd said, "There's nothing left
for us, not even martyrdom."
You smiled:
"At least stick to political
philosophy. Remember,
literature's too easy."

You'd smile again to see me
seven years later,
wintering in Florida
between a set of Eighteenth
Century novels and the sea.
A morning swim,
a day of marginalia,
lazy ambles on the shore
in the late afternoon;
eight thousand miles
from where, last night
a little after twelve,
a gunman called you to the door.

\*     \*     \*

This morning, when I came in
from the beach, a neighbor asked,
"You're from South Africa,
did you catch the news
about a doctor killed there,
Richard Tanner; the name
mean anything to you?"

So rapid the flood of it—
not medical doctor, *Turner*,
Richard, you . . . and the voice
from somewhere in the sudden
darkness, "Yes, Turner.
Did I upset you?"—
the premonition
must have gathered here for years.

You sat among us on the floor
translating Althusser,
barefoot, jeans, a pale blue shirt,
your black-rimmed lenses doubling
the light, the red shock of your hair.
At some slight turn of argument
your freckled hands followed
the actual phrasing in the air.
"I know it's difficult in this country,
but we've got to think more clearly
than the State allows."

Three years later, you were banned;
neither to be published
nor quoted in any form.
Forbidden to teach.

*       *       *

Long after midnight,
walking through the pines
into a thin sea wind,
startled as each line of water
shatters in the dark,
I half-prepare to meet you
further up the shore;
as though your dying meant
they'd only driven you out
to lead a half-life
here in the wind, this walk
between the water and pines
of another country.

Richard, if I keep to words,
believing nothing in our history
will make this right,
will what I say at last
be difficult enough
for you?

# PRETORIA

NOTE  *J. G. Strijdom, Prime Minister of South Africa, 1954–58. Paul Kruger, leader of the Boers during the war against the British, 1899–1902.*

In this city of magistrates,
even the jacarandas have ceded
pride of place to the architecture
of Republic Square, where stone,
cement and brass uphold an attitude
no change of light or hue was meant to mellow.
From its concrete bowl,
the bust of Strijdom stares
across the plaza to where laborers,
obedient to a rhythm of their own,
attend the pavement of the Opera House
until its surface offers up an image of themselves.

Up Church Street, Paul
Kruger, father of his nation,
sets a swollen jaw against the wind.
In low relief against his pedestal
a brazen hour of glory: Kruger
in his top hat calling
burghers to the "freedom fight."
Now, only the men in overalls,
the women in blankets on the yellow
winter grass are within distance
of his call. In knots of twos and threes,
their shadows pooled and lengthening,
they wait for night.

# TRANSVAAL: UNDER FROST

Too early for room-service,
we hunch over coffee in the lobby,
warm our hands and slip out
to the car as young newspaper
boys untie their bundles.

Eastward from Pretoria, the road
drops to a low mauve line of mist—
Machadodorp, the Kruger National Park,
and Mozambique—while all around
the pale lowveld gleams

dead-still apart from wispy
vapors drifting from cattle
as they breathe, or drop dung.
Past Witbank, bands of grey bleach
to a backlight for the stubble

of maize and thin, transparent scurf,
the occasional low thorn tree,
and now a windmill thawing
quietly—each token of an unseen
motion as of seasons undersoil.

A quickening motion no less in the people
we pass, the *Sotho* men with sticks,
the shrouded figures huddling over fires,
children running, hands in pockets
against the cold, their bare feet falling

softly on the light dirt margins
of the road. Behind them,
like struck chords, the fences tremble
where they clambered through,
a splinter of the sun on every barb.

# MACHADODORP

NOTE   *Machadodorp, a town in the Eastern Transvaal. Blerry, a pronunciation of bloody.*

Ox-heavy, leaning over the half-door
of our room, our farmer-hotelier
said, "Look, you need the background
of the thing. Before we came,
these blacks lived by a rule of fear:

no such thing as justice, no religion.
Think of Shaka's witch-hunts,
skewering men and women
to make the people fear his power.
Without us, they'd still be children

throwing assegais and spears
at one another in the bush. Don't
talk to me about who owns this land;
we built it up, we'll keep it—hell,
my family's worked this farm for eighty years!

But we can talk tonight, I'm off
to wash my hands—I've just been fixing up
the blerry pump." He smiles, holds up
a filthy hand, "Fresh trout with home-made
sauce for supper." And he stumps off.

It's hard to breathe. We step into
the early evening chill,
out past the hotel grounds,
farm-workers' huts of mud
and corrugated iron, on through

a gate into the sweet tambookie
grass, its reed-like spears
lining the path. The ground is thick
with dew. Around us, open contours
of this cattle and wheat country

25

play out to each soft
amber range, a low horizon
broken only by a line
of smoke, a stand of blue-gums
in a darkening cleft.

Before dusk, in a hollow
in the grass, I find a wire rod
tied to an iron wheel, cold to the touch,
a young cowherd's discarded toy.
And as I walk back, seeing the shadow

of our circling host
fall on our table, "How's the trout, hey, just
like Paradise?" I work the wheel until it loosens,
spins again; and then I let it drop,
my fingers wet now, streaked with rust.

## GIRAFFE

In an open jeep we
ease through the windless
quiet of a riverine forest
before dusk, searching
for animals, until
even the silent fall
of a thin acacia leaf,
or the small adjustments
of a bird among its feathers
become instinct with a far-off
scent of kudu, buffalo,
impala, moving in herds
toward the baffling
wire fences in the east.

A mile from camp, a crash
of branches and a thud among
the bushes spin us toward
a high, uprooted ebony
half-glimpsed as it overturns
through trees
but in the instant
disentangles
with a bound to lope clear
as a quivering bull giraffe!

Stunned, we know only
that we've come for this quick
leap of the senses
free as any creature
of these parts, the hoofbeats
entering the blood,
the shock of breathlessness
surviving as the taut
giraffe lapses to stillness,
balancing the dappled reach

of neck and haunches,
the elaborate play of hexagons
like a rippling wall,
and now, above a swirl
of dust, the shy half-floating
movement of the head,
inviting us to what
terrain still here between
the animal and ourselves?

# THE LIONS

Nightfall. The last warm air has lifted.
In the west, the outlined scar
of the Drakensberg seeps into the dark.
We take our bearings from the low star
of the Southern Cross, and peer at Jupiter,
its moon just visible through binoculars
if I could steady my hand—less cold
than nervous now we're tracking lions.
Our ranger has begun to talk.
Perhaps the darkness leads him to this
now we're each almost invisible.

"Of all wild animals, for me
only the predator is truly wild.
The fear it generates, a lion's
encircled by it, near-fearless himself,
dead center." Briefly his teeth glimmer.
"To study lions you must know
one from another, the distinguishing marks,
torn ears, whiskers, scars.
You have to get up close."

We ford the river on a shallow
underwater ledge. I lean out
to dip my hand in the eddy
at our wheels, and as we drive
through long grass on the far bank,
air cold on my wrist, he tells of facing
lion charges alone, on foot,
to within seven yards.

"As it moves, I draw an imaginary line,
a firing threshold, at say twenty yards,
but as the lion clenches then uncoils to charge,
everything slows down under pounding pressure—
dust hangs in the air, the lion looms,
shoulders bulging, legs straight out,

the head all jaw, ears back,
the belly swaying side to side
with every bound; and I redraw the line
at fifteen, then at ten,
the rifle heavy in my arms,
the lion crossing yard by yard
as though I fell to meet it.
Then it stops and snarls,
backing off a few yards,
and I back off, slowly, one step,
then another, its gaze following me."

We're riding over broken ground
our headlamps dip and lurch.
Behind us, on a high jump-seat
the Zulu tracker, Michael,
sweeps a flashlight side to side
scanning the bush for eyes,
or dropping the light straight down
for tracks. Quietly, the ranger tells
of Michael's battle with an aging lion.
We lean forward, our eyes travelling
the dim outline of bushes, long grass,
thorn-tree branches overhead.

"We'd sent him with his wife
to ready a campsite for a visiting group.
Clean up the place, air out the bungalow,
make beds. She was collecting firewood
in the trees beyond the clearing
when he heard her scream.
He snatched an iron pipe,
broke through the underbrush
and saw a black-maned lion
dragging at the bloody curled-up
bundle of his wife, her knees
drawn to her chest, right arm flung
overhead. Yelling, he hit the lion
across the spine and drew him off.

His wife was moaning, her left side
clawed open, arm wrenched
from the socket. Michael hauled
her toward the servants'
hut behind the bungalow,
every few seconds dropping her,
flailing the pipe to draw the lion
further off, then dragging her
a few yards closer to the hut.

Inside, he crouched over the threshold,
only the lower half of the doorway
shut by a broken two-leaf door,
the lion plunging up, and Michael
striking with the pipe, jabbing
with an old coke-bottle he'd picked up.
He couldn't barricade the door,
two windows had no panes, and the lion
kept coming after the smell of blood.
Once, he smashed it over the eye,
and as it reeled off in a daze
he tore his clothing into tourniquets
and with a blanket roped his wife
into the eaves. He hacked a mattress
into halves and jammed each window,
hanging his greatcoat in the door.
Whenever the lion leaped,
he'd beat it through the coat.

This went on into the night,
Michael guarding in the dark
while the lion roared and lunged
at the doorway. Michael's wife
hung from the roof without a moan,
no longer answering to her name.
Unsure if she were still alive,
he couldn't step back from the door
until, near dawn, the lion
clawed away the coat and dragged it
out of sight beyond the trees.

The woman lived;
three months in a hospital
outside Pretoria, then we
brought her back. Lost almost
all use of her arm, still limps.
But we kept her on—
in fact she made your beds."

He doesn't pause, neither for shame
nor admiration. "We found the lion
three days later, dead, a few miles
from the site. Too old to hunt,
he probably hadn't killed for weeks
before attacking Michael's wife.
He'd disgorged pieces of the coat
near where he lay."

We ride in silence, seeing little—
only a timid bushbuck blinded
by our lights—but then
the quick alarm call of a bird
breaks near the river,
the *loerie's* "gway, goway,"
heard now for the first time.
A few yards further, lion tracks
lead through thicker bush.
The branches crack beneath our wheels,
screech along the metal as we pass.
Beyond a gully, we jolt forward
as the ranger stops dead,
sucks his breath and motions
with his head toward the long grass
thirty feet away. At first nothing;
then the blank glare of its eyes
returning our headlights, the low-sunk
head barely distinguished in the grass.
The ranger lifts his rifle,
takes a cartridge between thumb
and forefinger, slides it in the breech,

and bolts it home.
Gun in one hand, wheel in the other,
he nudges the jeep another wheel-turn
forward, and cuts the engine.

And now it stands,
a large dark-colored male
emerging from the grass,
the head held low toward us.
In two bounds it could be
over us, or shot down;
but after a moment's stare,
a sudden blaze behind the mirror
of the eyes, it pads into the dark.

Later, riding back, I squint
against the rush of cold air,
seeing only the lion draw
me back to that original
lifting of its body from the grass,
that gaze. And closer now,
the lion lunging through a broken door,
my own arm jerking back
as though in sleep.
At camp, Michael brings
a paraffin lantern to each bungalow.
He looks down—no less awkward
at our sudden quietness
than we are—and then quickly
turns away across the dark compound,
his own lantern swinging
beside him as he walks.

## VALERIE

You've joined those
who cross the ocean after me,
arriving under dark,
the mute ones, visiting.

I understand the others,
tangled in the heart's own fear,
but you stood always
on the margin,

our vacation aunt each
winter down the coast,
the small town doctor's wife,
Aunt Val, or Aunty V,

ferrying us each day
from beach to tennis club—
the road through canefields
out of town.


One year, dazzled
by a motorcycle parked
outside the house,
all chrome and sunlight,

I, just ten, leaned up
to touch its handlebars,
and as I peered at the speedometer,
the yellow figures under glass,

90, 100, 110,
the bright exhaust pipe
burned into my leg for seconds
before I knew enough to tear away.

For days the massive blister
oozing through the gauze
was no match for your patience.
In the garden,

wild banana trees,
their wide leaves white
under the coastal salt,
the weak papaya branches

awkward in the wind,
a bougainvillea's
brilliant splash of crimson
over the chicken run,

I'm watching you unwind
another roll of gauze,
the scissors in your right hand,
safety pin between your lips.

Is it the manner of your death
that brings you back
these nights, your son beside you
at the wheel, the drunk accelerating

on a blind rise
coming at you with a violence
nothing in your life
had led you to suppose?


Once, though, as we drove home
from the beach, a cane-press worker
flagged us down, held up
the bloody ruin of his arm.

I remember your voice
seemed to shield us
from the raw pulp of the hand
held to the car window,

blood on the lowering glass,
the shattered bone laid
bare under the flesh.
You were speaking Zulu,

"Let me wrap your hand,
come with us to the hospital,
the doctor's there." It seems now
we were always frightened in that country.

I still turn to it with a child's fear.
—Valerie, if you could hear,
I'd say watch over us.
Watch over the dark coast.

## NEWS FROM HOME

I'm thinking of our garden roses
leaning heavily across the open gate
the week we parted—separate journeys,
yours to China, mine Morocco, Spain—
the distance closing now as I look backward
from the Spanish coast; the roses clustered
so blood-red, so densely, even now I see
thin cloth and flesh torn open
to a spread of gunshot wounds.

I still resist the image, call it forced,
though forced on me: that morning's news
of further killings in South Africa—
the armored cars parked where the township ends,
machine guns firing on a funeral march, scattered
bodies dragged away before the relatives could claim
more than a dark smear on the ground.

A garden's often been the site
in which we image our disasters;
why not blood-red roses ripping open
the sheer havoc at the heart
of what might be a love poem?

We'll be together in a week,
and yet I'm reaching toward those roses
with a need which, though I know
one of its names is love,
cannot be satisfied by the best
that holds or passes between any two of us.

The heavy blossoms turn their dark heads
horizontal to the ground.
If I could, I'd take them, cut them, shake them
free for you; if I thought that might
leave more than just the stems.
What grows about them gathers round us, too.
What moves between, what fills, what cannot hold,
however heavily it clots—is flowing here.

# PART III

# In These Mountains

# IN THESE MOUNTAINS

NOTE   *The Bushmen, or San, have sometimes been called "the first people of Southern Africa," or "the people of the eland"—eland being a specie of South African antelope with which they had a special affinity. During the nineteenth century, the Bushmen retreated to the deserts and mountains of Southern Africa, finding there a temporary refuge from the advance of recent settlers.*

*The surviving Bushmen of the desert now live mainly in the Kalahari Desert of Namibia and Botswana. Many live on reservations, and numbers of the men have been used by the South African Defence Force as trackers and soldiers in the guerrilla war along the borders of Namibia.*

*Of the mountain Bushmen, none survive. In 1872, a white commando group carried out a "punitive raid" against the last band, in the Drakensberg of Natal. It is said that this small band included a painter—cave-paintings being the only trace now left of the Bushmen in these parts.*

\*      \*      \*

Today in a German dictionary, I saw *elend*
And the heart in my breast turned over, it was—

It was a word one translates *wretched*.

—Randall Jarrell

Kung Bushmen call all strangers *zhu dole*, which means "stranger" but, literally, "dangerous person;" they call all non-Bushmen *zo si*, which means "animals without hooves," because, they say, non-Bushmen are angry and dangerous like lions and hyenas. But Kung Bushmen call themselves *zhu twa si*, the harmless people. *Twa* means "just" or "only" in the sense that you say: "It was just the wind" or "it is only me."

—Elizabeth Marshall Thomas

I remember mountain water running over stones
so smooth there is no sound—even with
the ear held close it runs as quietly as if
the stones had melted into water, into light.

In these mountains antelope still move freely,
blesbok, hartebees, the russet oribi on open ridges,
klipspringers near rock outcrops, heavy eland
browsing quietly on lower slopes, their bodies
honey-colored, merging with the grass.

In sandstone caves we'd find the eland painted
on the walls, some scratched over with initials,
others in the higher caves untouched.
Though we saw human figures running with the animals,
the paintings could have been deposited by the wind,
or water seeping through the stone for all we knew
of Bushmen: a kind of yellow pygmy,
I remember hearing as a child, they died out
naturally in these parts a century ago—
a people unadapted to the modern world.

Once though, on a four day ride, we camped
in a narrow cave, and as I spread my bedroll
under a ledge deep in the shelter I saw
small paintings dimly in the stone,
near-black images stirring in the last
firelight and smoke—a group of men
with heads of antelope, long masks with eland horns,
a spotted serpent on a winding vein of rock,
another figure like a praying mantis
spread for flight. And long before dawn
I woke cold in the darkness hearing
the hobbled horses stamp the grass,
the sound of wind, of water dripping
though I heard no rain, and the uncertain figures
moving in the low stone overhead.

*    *    *

"Master, you know that I sit waiting for the moon
to turn back for me, that I may return
to my place. That I may listen again
to my people's stories, which come from
a long way off. For here I have no stories.
But I truly think that I must only
await the moon, that I may tell my master
I feel this is the time when I should sit
among my fellow men, who walking meet their like.
They are listening to the stories there.
I must first cool my arms a little
that the tiredness may leave them,
waiting for a story—it may float into my ear."

*     *     *


Seven figures step in single file
out of the sandstone wall, stepping down
through cloudy patches of eroded stone,
some with a pole or stick held out to spread
the body's weight across the unseen path.

Travellers on migration, each cloaked
in a dark kaross, or hunters carrying a kill,
hump-backed, leaning slightly forward on
their slender legs, a part of each torso
dissolving into pale rock or cloud
then re-emerging. Shadowy figures burdened
and yet floating as they walk—the way
the dead might move, or spirits walking toward life.

*     *     *

"We set off before dawn, ten of us,
with two old Zulus ahead
following the Bushmen tracks in the frost.
They'd come on foot, poisoned the cattle,
then ridden away on horses stolen
from the farm. Two hours uphill
we found the horses, three dead,
one still kicking—each with little
arrows in the chest. From there
we lost the track, but followed a narrow
pass where some days back we'd seen
a group of eland running as if
startled by hunters higher up.
A mile from the sandstone cliffs
we tethered our horses and crept ahead,
each alone, holding a heavy
duffle-coat in case of arrows.
Crawling close to the ground—a swish
of dry grass as we moved, the smell
of it pressed under arms and knees.

"I was resting, head down, when
the first gun shattered, echoing back
down off the cliff, then a second,
and a Bushman rolling in a ball,
then two figures scrambling sideways
to the cave. I missed one, hard
to see his yellow body in the grass,
but the rest of us were firing,
some advancing on the cave;
and then we all closed in, the rifle
fire deafening against the rock.

"Further back in the half-light:
the bullet caught him in the chest,
spun him against the wall—
a little man, his skin all wrinkled,
I remember how his hands
spread on the stone for a second
till he crumpled like a leather rag,
his eyes wide open, a strangled
sucking sound down in the throat.

"The cave was thick with smoke, the light
from outside swirling in a heavy shaft,
our men looming in it, Bushmen
scattered on the ground.
All dead except for one old man
someone had shot in the rump to see
if all that extra flesh could hurt.
We couldn't tell, though it bled fast
in a thick pool, the Bushman lying
on his side and weeping without
sound, arms up to hide his face."

*     *     *

The wind blows through a small reed island
in the mountain pool. There in the shadowed water
Kaggen hid his son-in-law Kwammanga's
offcast leather shoe, returning every day
to watch it grow. He'd sing to it,
trilling his tongue the way reeds quiver
in the wind, a quiet clicking as they lean together,
the way the hunters used to sing,
calling "Kwammanga's leather shoe,
Kwammanga's shoe." Until the sandal grew
to a young eland and came into his arms.
And he would gently rub its head with honey,
rubbing its young flanks with honeycomb.

Kwammanga, missing three days' honey,
followed Kaggen to the mountain pool.
He lay under a long kaross, still
as a low stone near the water's edge,
hearing "Kwammanga's leather shoe," with the soft
clicking sound. And through a chink in the kaross,
squinting against the light, he saw pale legs
step from the reeds, the wet hooves
glittering, an orange-ochre flank, a soft
dewlap beneath the throat, black horns pointing
straight back from the head, the nostrils
quivering. And Kaggen now with honey
in his hands, smoothing the eland's hair.

Alone, Kwammanga crept from his kaross.
At his low call the reeds stirred and the eland
trotting in the shallow water took
Kwammanga's arrow in the neck. When an eland
leaps the weight moves through the body
as a ripple runs across a pool, or cloth
unfurls when shaken in the wind. When Kaggen
called at dusk only the wind moved
through the reeds and then a nonsense song,
Kwammanga singing as he turned the carcass
on a bed of leaves, laying the parts aside:
the intestine cleaned out with a stick, the gall,
the rumen, and the heart; the blood collected
in a pit lined with the eland's hide.

The eland's heart, the hide bowl of dark blood.
Kwammanga churned until blood spattered
the ground, where each drop slithered off—a worm,
a long red lizard, or a snake. But Kaggen
threw heart's fat into the bowl, taking the spindle
in his hands. The blood grew yellowish,
and from each drop an eland fled into the hills.
And Kaggen followed like a wind moving
among them calling, quivering his tongue.
So that the hunters asked have you not heard
his song when the eland start and run?
And as they hunted they would ask,
have you not heard him crying in the wind?

*     *     *

I've been returning this way since a child,
the road up through the Valley of a Thousand Hills
into the Midlands, climbing to the Drakensberg,
I and my sister in the back seat, pitching
cheap sweets to the children, heart-shaped candy
eight for a penny at trading stores,
each piece stamped with a Zulu phrase we never
thought to understand. Was it the beauty
that distracted us, high blue-gums
along the road, leaves shivering in cascades
over the pale trunks, sweet resin in the air?
Cool air, open grasslands slanting toward
the mountains, placid cattle with their heads down
motionless, as though drinking the grass.
And passing far more quickly than the farms,
an occasional ring of huts like hives
in the contour of a hill, a straggle of half-dressed
children in the yard, chickens, dogs,
all sliding by, the cowherd boys barefoot
in winter, stick legs under long thin jackets,
pockets flapping at their hips. We waved,
but even they were scenery; the women balancing
a body's length of firewood overhead—
eight hours' forage, though to us they moved
with an easy dream-like motion through the fields.

Flying back this time, I watched the stars
change as we dropped down Africa, until I followed
a mountain track, the dry clay crumbling underfoot.
In a side-gully three fishermen tore at soft
translucent creatures in the pale earth,
spearing them with slender metal spikes.
Near formless embryos budding worm-like limbs,
aware enough only to writhe defenseless
as the metal slid through organs pulsing
faintly visible below the flesh. The wrench
and squeal, the bloody spikes, the mounds left squirming
half-dead under the sun, one seen from close up

bleeding from the membrane of its mouth—
still closer, till I woke, my head
sliding in sweat against the window blind.

*　　*　　*

Pale ochre, winter-rose, the long grass
at my shins, taller clumps knee-high with a mat
of last year's growth entangling each foot
as it feels for hidden cavities or mounds
of shadowed earth—knees, hips, shoulders
following as the body stores
the changing form and pressure of the ground.

Above a narrow trail leading to the caves,
a hazy mesh of stalks, thin wisps,
filaments in a lit tangle of static
where grass tips seethe into the light.
Not seen, then seen, a tuft of grass turns
in a flickered gathering of mass to the stillness
of an eland's head, horns back, the ears
almost transparent, soft grey muzzle scenting
to where I stand long after, caught
in that first sighting as the eland
works away uphill browsing the low
*mchicha* bushes soundlessly until
it disappears into the slope.

*　　*　　*

In a high buttress above the valley,
sandstone sediment eroded deep into the lower face,
light filters through thin yellowwood leaves
to the shelter walls, the boulders fallen from the roof,
the sandy floor; a light soft as the sound
of water lifted up and echoing in the cave.

Outside the entrance, a high wire fence—
"Vandals," the Parks Board had explained.
"We've also made a small museum in the cave."
The bored attendant in a smart safari suit,
"Saniboni" and "Unjani"
(almost my last remaining Zulu words)
greets us with tape cassette in hand,
"The Background of the Bushmen:
their life-style and art."

"A tough nomadic race, they settled
here when farmers occupied the elands'
grazing in the Midlands of Natal."
Wax models, life size, crudely sculpted—
a Bushman lying on a frayed kaross,
his weight on hip and elbow, belly falling
slantwise to the dusty hide, a slender
arrow held in one hand, with a length
of uncoiled thread poised in the other.
". . . cunning livestock raiders but quite innocent,
they couldn't understand such things as ownership.
They thought of cattle in the same light
as wild animals." A woman, young but wrinkled,
flesh moulded into folds the color of dust,
a child beside her on the ground,
an ostrich shell, a pair of dancing rattles
"from dried cocoons of pupae used for poison arrows.
They'd fill them with bone fragments,
bind them to their feet." And the tape
runs on with gods and legends, Kaggen
and the Moon, star spirits—myths reduced
to sacrifice and resurrection, painting
as the expiation or replenishment
for what the hunters killed. A thread of Bushman
music follows as we turn aside.
The attendant smiles, returning to his chair.

Unframed, running freely on the walls,
a herd of eland moves across the stone,
small figures as one sees them in the distance,
some receding, others nearer
leaping, heads thrown back, each body in a long
repeating curve, the soft V of the neck,
the mounded ridge above the shoulders sinking
to a long swayed back rising again
over the rump; the flanks dun-red,
the underflanks and legs bone-white
so that each animal appears uplifted, floating
on the stone. Near them, human figures
even smaller, running in full stride
with sticks and bows, here circling an eland bleeding
on the ground, hooves in the air, pale head
wrenched to one side. Others looming in the mist,
each shrouded in a long kaross over
the shoulders blanketing the hips, dark
as dark blood, charcoal, burned manganese.

And here on this side wall the hunter's moon,
the white-haired moon, holding her weapons
in her hands, a quiver slung across
her back, five arrows needle-thin,
her gleaming belly flecked with ochre,
darkening legs turned outward at the knee.

"O Moon, give me the face
with which you, having died, return."

                    *       *       *


Shadows slant across the escarpment
rising like a wave drawn back
2000 feet above the hills. Below,
the Bushman's River cuts between the mountain
grasslands, broken water glittering downstream
darkening in pools, a constant high-pitched
rush between the valley slopes, the hollow
clonk of boulders on the river bed.

One step at a time into the water,
ankles, knees burning then numb in the fast
current tugging me down, each hand
groping for a stone. Now outstretched
tightly in a submerged trough of basalt,
feet braced on a boulder, river thrashing
neck and shoulders, breaking overhead
to wash away down-valley in a churning mass.

At dusk high over the river looking toward
the escarpment silhouette, thinking of the road
back to the coast. Far down, a herd
moves slowly grazing a narrow spread of green.
They move like ears of wheat or wild grass,
pausing, gathering, moving on, moving away.

Waiting in a raw wind on the open hill
a stubble of burned grass underfoot,
the soot thick on my shoes, I look upwind
once more, losing the hard edge of each mountain,
seeing only the painted figures step
from the walls into the night, the hunters and
their herds disintegrating in a cloud of unlit dust.
And now a small form huddled on
a sandstone floor, eroded and yet stirring
as from sleep, lifting the head, the wide
misshapen mouth dark as the shadows in the cave,
dark as the night air flowing everywhere
among these mountains blowing empty, hollowing
the hills without a sound—no bird cry,
no river sound, no spirits travelling quickly
with their quivers under the cold drift of stars,
their bone-chip rattles and their voices
streaming in the darkness and the wind.

# PART IV

# San Vio

# VILLANELLE

You take your sorrow with you when you leave.
However wide the sea or sky between,
the journey's end will bring you no reprieve.

Stand at the rail, and as you gaze believe
the past drifts backward on the long wake's sheen.
You take your sorrow with you when you leave.

Look forward, sea wind on your face, conceive
with gladness the imaginary scene
the journey's end will bring you, the reprieve

now holding out its soft-lit valley to receive
you weary in its arms. No less keen
you take your sorrow with you when you leave.

Whatever drives or beckons, nothing you achieve
keeps back the pain: you might have seen
the journey's end would bring you no reprieve.

Unless the heart at last deceives
the low wind calling to the heart's own scene,
you take your sorrow with you when you leave.
The journey's end will bring you no reprieve.

# ARLES: THE BULLS

Bull after bull, I kept one
hand on the stone,
thinking of the cool quarries
of Gaul laid open
centuries ago for this—

a matador bungling the coup
de grâce more
clumsily each time, the swordblade
buckling on raw
bone, the bull gashed, prodded

to distraction by the picadors
and now forced
kneeling to the sand, gasping for air,
the crowd poised
swaying like a rotten harvest in the glare.

For the space of one slow death I walked
under the dark
arena, touching each stone-barrelled
archway as they took
another bull out to be felled.

When the crowd drifted away downhill
the bulls were hauled
on chains, hung up and hoisted to a cart,
the block and tackle
groaning as the winch drew taut.

His back to me, a man stood
sluicing the concrete,
blood thinning to water, disappearing
through an iron grate
set in the ground. Lying

awake that night, I heard it running
through the sewers
under us, and saw it fall,
the watery bloodstream slipping
through the dark under us all.

# THE RED CAVE

A path threaded the terraces, crossed
a narrow stream, then straggled upslope
into rock and weeds, a slide of dry
shale underfoot. Thin air.

Heads down, we first heard his high
whistling laugh, the small
Ladakhi boy, face like a waning
moon, half-grin and nervous eyes.

A waif, scarecrow-awry, crooning
"One rupee, one pen?" holding
a fistful of wildflowers pulled
from a terrace hedge—

Himalayan lavender, wild
iris, wild few-petalled roses,
tight white orchids
with a bitter smell—

our shifty joker, beggar, guide,
pointing to the dark caves overhead,
already ushering us toward a
zig-zag ledge.


Inside, images of Buddha
and his Boddhisatvas multiplied
in squares within a square on every wall,
the figures seated meditating

in the dark, identical
save where the hands in differing
gestures seemed to counter-poise
each body's stillness in its frame.

Peace at the heart of peace.
But the red cave? High in the cliff,
its dark mouth smeared with red,
an eyrie, inaccessible,

too sheer to climb, though a wild
stretch from a nearby overhang may
reach the loose stones near the lip,
if they'd bear weight. The boy won't try.

Danger or taboo? Looking at the drop,
you mutter "Local wisdom.
Go on, I'll wait for you." No rope,
on hands and knees, the valley

narrowing below. Above, a side-slope
sucks back to the sky. A spidery
sideways dangle, once,
twice, feeling for the stones

then wavering for balance
as they slide and take hold.
The reach up for the cave mouth,
and a hoist into the dark.


A smell of dust. Old smoke.
The bare cave wall beneath
decaying frescoes.
Further in the gloom, emerging

from the hollows
of the hill itself, the god or demon,
lapis, night-blue, almost indigo,
embracing his bare lover

lunar white, seen from below,
his arms around her, blue hands
spread across her thighs, her
legs splayed out to either side

hurdling the air, as though for her
this joining were a flight
across night air, a long run
even at the heart of penetration.

Lust, or the soul at one
with wisdom? Undeciding, drawn
to them as though I too were
moving on the wall,

a channel breaking somewhere
flowing toward these figures, held
by them, dissolving, running on—
no longer gods,

but man and woman in the quick of genesis,
a wheel of limbs set moving
in a fluent pulse already
beating at the body's core.


Beyond the Indus, snow-peaks soften
in the summer dusk, the village
settles in a thickening pall.
Out of the dark, below the barley fields,

a mother's high-pitched call;
and now the boy's reply, a young owl's cry
too thin to reach the village. Again
the mother's lingering call.

We quicken our steps along the hillstream,
following the sound of waters mingling
downward over their rough bed,
the doubtful homing cry.

# SAN VIO

*Where is he who tears off the husks for you and me?*
  —Whitman

Or how we followed our own shadows
falling forward on the wet-lit calle,
sound of rain and footsteps, black umbrellas
over us, till later as we lay in bed,
the Gesuati bells swung slow
colliding almost randomly, like sea bells
not quite softened in the rain.

To be recalled when lost. As if already lost.
As if we live in memory even now—
a slip of oarlight on the dark canal.

I'd watch them row, the oar snug in its open lock,
the blade not breaking water—stirring,
slipping forward flat under the surface, twisting back,
the weight of water balancing the man.


Or the wellstone in this campo, its worn angel
wingless in the merest blur of an angelic form,
too smooth, too far from its original relief;
a solid lid clamped to the rim,
dull metal, olive-brown to black,
the waters of San Vio buried in the shaft.

A city of false starts and aberrations,
narrow alleys changing course beyond direction,
like this passageway outside a garden
hidden by decaying walls whose colors
draw the eye through centuries, the ear half-lulled
by lapping water, to a dark dead-end.
Mossed steps disappearing in a back canal—
white under green, then green.
The water swallowing stone.

And all the while unsure not only of direction
but of tense, losing us each moment
in the future perfect or the past:
after I, you, all this will have been,
how long will I have waited to have given you
this shadow of an old Venetian rose?

*　　*　　*

Turning listlessly through every angle,
hoping some forgotten grit might catch
the light, something undigested, swallowed whole.
Returning to this city of stolen sanctity
diffused to colored stone, wet steps,
palaces carved to distraction riding
their own shimmer effortlessly
as we float or walk—the dream indifferent
to its dreamers, or to what may gather
in side canals, a worm of lamplight
slithering in black water, bottles bobbing,
air trapped in the glass.

Here five years ago, I first dreamed
of a dying man beneath my childhood home—
a black man dying in the unlit cellar.
As a child I'd seen him pass beneath my window,
watched him tug his short-brimmed hat
as he'd step from the alley to the street.
And once (or was this, too, imagined?) a quick glance
toward me at the window bars, his finger
pointing for a moment, and the whisper
"white cockroach, white fish. . . ."
For years I listened for his passing,
watched for his face at the wrought-iron bars.

Now, lying on a hessian mat,
a canvas flight bag at his side,
the sort employers discard to domestics
after each new flight, a sick or wounded fugitive
afraid of questioning, afraid I'd see

the bandage crusted to his chest.
Crouched beside him with a flashlight,
stooped under the floorboards of the house,
did I agree to let him die in secrecy?

Not the harshest dream of home—
the hooded men heard crashing
through the glass doors of the house;
the death of friends who chose to stay,
one shot through the window of his home,
one driven all night naked in a van,
beaten to death against a prison wall.
Waking this time less in horror
or in vengeful anger than in grief,
the wished for reconciliation come too late.

                    *    *    *


So that dreaming in this city—whose
constantly inconstant rocking soothes
the ear, whose wash of light on marble
and still water intervenes like a soft film
of ease or pleasure on the eye—recalls
my country, perhaps explains this stooping
now with fever, back-ache, fascinated
with the labor of concealment rotting in the bone.

(For exiles or expatriates there are times
when all they left, by time and distance grown
immaterial, will nonetheless compact
as to a residue that will not be dissolved,
a silt that rises in the blood, that spreads
at large in the adopted world, and *is* that world,
beyond a personal disease, the bitter bread, the stairs.
The times when it is clear they have evaded nothing,
turned from nothing . . .)

Up the marble stairs, the twisting banister,
on through the mottled mirror doors,
Murano chandeliers, ancestral portraits,

we stood in the palazzo after midnight,
champagne glass in hand, guests by default
commandeered by an expansive host,
that weekend's tenant, telling
how he'd "fucked the German Bank."
How life was neither art, nor love, nor intellect,
but *steel*. And as he raged against the "benders"—
those who hid the difference between races,
genders, rich and poor—himself
the banker-impresario of what he called
the European avant-garde,
around us leaned his coterie
exhaling in five languages, the rearguard
whose vocation was to give form
to the end of an unending era.

From the velvet balcony we looked down
at the stonework running fluent
over unseen pilings driven in the marsh.
A crab clung to the landing,
pale in lamplight, green weeds
swaying over its unmoving claws.

"Don't be so nervous," our host said
before we left. "Don't take it seriously."

*   *   *

Crossing toward Torcello on the flat lagoon,
following huddled pilings chained or banded
head to blackened head,
a spread of weed below the water mark.

"A place emerged among the marshes . . .
home of fugitives." Along a thin canal,
the feathery tamarisks, from a distance ashen,
salt-burned or sun-bleached; but closer,
close enough to break a sprig
as we slid by, I found it pale with seed.

Though more at ease with the empty circle
of the baptistry, its pillar stumps
and fallen capitals sunk in the scum,
the long marsh grass, a cavity of bricks.


Inside, familiar aisles and walls,
the blue mosaic mother of God descending
the high curve of the golden apse, the Christ-child
in her lap, the twelve apostles
whom the guide book, erring into poetry,
has "alternating in the low folds
of the priestly planet"—as if the only words
to match that beauty were a mistranslation.

On the far wall, Judgment Day,
cornpoppies littering the ground of Paradise,
a guardian cherub, red wings crammed with eyes,
the damned thrust in the fire, the lustful
with the gluttonous, the proud and indolent, a serpent
sliding through the sockets of each skull.


Following a track through grass, a stench of refuse
stacked in black bags on the far canal,
drawn now more to brick and its eroding shades
than to mosaic, the outer walls of the cathedral
weathered to siena, amber, salmon, red,
a streak of lime-green lichen on the campanile,
rust stains from the window bars; the stone
itself scabbed, porous, powdery to touch
but each piece as if moulded by the weight
of the surrounding bricks to its own strength and size.

Above a ditch on the near side,
windowslabs stood open on stone hinges,
solid windows, ivory veined with grey,
each fastened to the wall by rusted stays.

Recrossing the lagoon past shattered
island shrines, the windowslabs seen hanging
in the half-dream of a stone swung open
to sheer sky over the water, like that section
of the Judgment Wall, the dead called
from the sea, hauled upward by the sound
of horns, the music moving through the water
to the figures swimming up through wavering
bands of blue and white, some still struggling
from the monster's mouth. And the words *Porta*
*Salutis, Maris Astrum* chiselled in mosaic,
with the script of Christ, *Non piger ad lapsum*
*sed flentis proximus adsum*—I am not far
from the offender, but I am nearest the penitent.

And yet how far from penitence this daydream
of the opening stone, the lifted lid of sea
with a figure now emerging vertically,
white drapes unbandaging, a naked figure
climbing upward through receding choirs of space.

The merest fantasy of relief, too weak
for hope; unless those burning on the wall
and these seen waking from the dead could be
the vicious and the fallen of this world
judged now, or rising as from sleep.

Passing through the campo at nightfall,
a smell of old stone moldering to slime,
the unseen well-shaft sucking to a clown-white mask
flat in the water—two holes sunk for eyes,
a dark smudge at the mouth—

unmoving, till a wellhead pebble drops
to its explosion shivering up the column,
circles of lit water scattered
like a shoal of pale fish breaking outward,
leaping and collapsing at the walls.

\*     \*     \*

Along the Rio da San Vio,
in the Fondamenta da Ca' Bragadin,
the water, quiet and yet tidal,
laps at one moored boat and then another,
like a late night conversation
drifting back and forth between those close
to sleep, who, intimate, half-whisper
half-murmur a partial phrase and yet
are understood. The black-hulled boats
moored separately, edging a little way
toward each other in the dark.